Kalpana Chawla

Published in the United States of America by Cherry Lake Publishing Group
Ann Arbor, Michigan
www.cherrylakepublishing.com

Reading Adviser: Beth Walker Gambro, MS, Ed., Reading Consultant, Yorkville, IL
Book Designer: Jennifer Wahi
Illustrator: Jeff Bane

Photo Credits: © Rizwan_Sayyed/Shuttershock, 5; © Mohammad Shahnawaz/Shuttershock, 7; © happy photo/Shuttershock, 9; © baipooh/Shuttershock, 11; © Graeme Dawes/Shuttershock, 13; © NASA/GPN-2003-00072, 15, 22; © NASA/STS-087-357-022, 17, 23; © NASA/S107E05001, 19; © NASA/KSC-02pd1954, 21; Cover, 1, 8, 10, 12, Jeff Bane; Various frames throughout, © Shutterstock Images

Cherry Lake Press is an imprint of Cherry Lake Publishing Group.

Library of Congress Cataloging-in-Publication Data has been filed and is available at catalog.loc.gov

Printed in the United States of America
Corporate Graphics

table of contents

My Story 4

Timeline 22

Glossary 24

Index 24

About the author: When not writing, Dr. Virginia Loh-Hagan serves as the director of the Asian Pacific Islander Desi American (APIDA) Center at San Diego State University. She identifies as Chinese American and is committed to amplifying APIDA communities. She lives in San Diego with her very tall husband and very naughty dogs.

About the illustrator: Jeff Bane and his two business partners own a studio along the American River in Folsom, California, home of the 1849 Gold Rush. When Jeff's not sketching or illustrating for clients, he's either swimming or kayaking in the river to relax.

I was born in 1962 in India. I had an older brother. I also had two older sisters.

I picked my name. My name means "idea."

What does your name mean?

I saw a plane when I was 3.
After that, I knew I wanted to fly.

I joined flying clubs. I watched planes with my dad. I studied **engineering** in college.
I **graduated**.

I moved to the United States to continue studying. I studied in Texas and Colorado. I fell in love and got married.

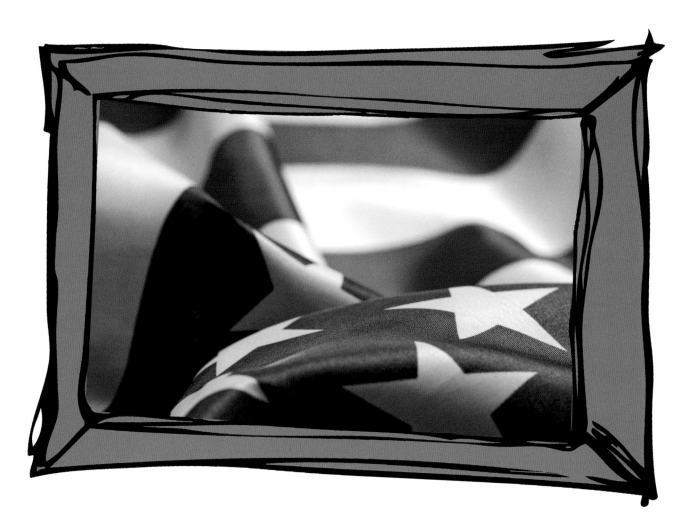

I worked for **NASA**. I applied to be an **astronaut**. I was denied. I applied again and succeeded.

What are your dreams?

I flew to space. I circled Earth.
I did this 252 times on my first
mission.

I had a second mission. I went back to space. But something happened on my trip back to Earth.

My **shuttle** blew up. I died in 2003. My **legacy** lives on. I was the first Indian American woman in space. I spent 30 days in space.

What would you like to ask me?

1994

1960

Born
1962

Died
2003

1997

2060

glossary

astronaut (A-struh-nawt) a person who is trained to travel in a spacecraft

engineering (en-juh-NEER-ing) the use of science and math to design or make things

graduated (GRA-juh-way-tuhd) received an academic degree or diploma

legacy (LEH-guh-see) something handed down from one generation to another

mission (MIH-shuhn) a flight by an aircraft or spacecraft to perform a specific task

NASA (NAH-suh) National Aeronautics and Space Administration

shuttle (SHUH-tuhl) a spacecraft designed to transport people and cargo between Earth and space

index

astronaut, 14

engineering, 10

fly, 8, 10

India, 4
Indian American, 20

married, 12
mission, 16, 18

NASA, 14

plane, 8, 10

space, 16, 20
study, 10, 12